THE PRESIDENT
and the SUPREME COURT

New Deal to Watergate

JOHN D. LEES

British Association for American Studies

First published 1980

First Reprinting 1982

ISBN 0 9504601 3 3

ACKNOWLEDGMENTS

We are grateful to the BBC Hulton Picture Library, London, for permission to reproduce the photographs used as the frontispiece and on the back cover; and to the Photographic Laboratory, United States International Communication Agency, London, for providing the photographs of inauguration ceremonies reproduced on the front cover and on page 31. We also appreciate the kindness of the Pittsburgh *Post Gazette*, and of Mr. Hungerford, in permitting us to reproduce the cartoon on page 17.

Printed by Peterson Printers, 12 Laygate, South Shields. Tel: (0632) 563493.

Contents

Charles Evans Hughes, Chief Justice of the United States, 1930-1941.

1: The Constitutional Legacy

Every four years on Inauguration Day a newly elected President accepts the burdens and duties of the office. The ceremony is presided over by the Chief Justice of the United States, who requires the President to take the oath or affirmation set out in the Constitution:

I do solemnly swear (or affirm) that I will faithfully execute the office of President of the United States, and will to the best of my ability, preserve, protect and defend the Constitution of the United States.

The President, of course, is taking up probably the most powerful elected political office in history — and the most frustrating, impossible and man-killing job.[1] The Chief Justice provides a marked contrast. Unlike the new President, his name and face will often be unfamiliar to a majority of the many millions who nowadays watch an inauguration ceremony, yet his role in the ceremony and in the workings of the political system may be at least as important as that of any President.

At the Inauguration the Chief Justice is symbolically the more significant figure, for it is he who invests the new chief executive with legitimacy and constitutional authority. In his routine capacity, moreover, he can dictate the terms upon which the President exercises his power — as did the Chief Justice pictured on the front cover of the pamphlet at the 1973 Inauguration. Such authority derives from the fact that he presides over the Supreme Court of the United States — a body of nine appointed Justices who have been characterized in turn as guardians of the Constitution, and as undemocratic and irresponsible old men.

The role of the Supreme Court in American government is both less visible and less understood than that of the President. First and foremost, it is a court of law and the highest court in the American judicial system. When we think of judges, we normally think of persons who are impartial, neutral and *nonpolitical*, and indeed this aura of impartiality is projected in many of the formal activities of the Justices of the Supreme Court. They wear long black robes, their proceedings are conducted with formality, dignity and decorum, and meetings to discuss pending cases are conducted in secret. Nevertheless the Supreme Court is, in comparison with other judicial bodies throughout the world, a powerful political institution. From the beginning it has been involved in the policy-making processes of American government. As a court of law operating under a written constitution its impact is judicial, but in performing this role it may make decisions which have direct implications for public policy, for example by invalidating a decision of a President. To this extent its influence on public policy is different from that of the Congress or the President, and the nature of its authority makes it a difficult institution to comprehend. It is the intention here to aid such understanding by analysing its relationship with the Presidency in the years 1933 to 1974.

The rationale for concentrating on this period is a simple one. The New Deal and the Presidency of Franklin Roosevelt produced a fundamental change in the American political process, affecting the national government as a whole and the role of the President in particular. World War II and the realities of the Cold War furthered the concentration of authority and responsibility in the executive, and provided the foundation for what Arthur M. Schlesinger, Jr., has described as "the imperial Presidency".[2] Watergate, and the attempted cover-up, produced a political crisis which again affected the Presidency — and the future role of the chief executive — in ways which are still difficult to assess with precision. [3] At critical moments in these developments Supreme Court decisions were of great significance, and they raised crucial issues regarding the scope and the limits of executive and judicial authority.

In order to appreciate the importance of Court decisions in the development of the modern Presidency since 1933, it is necessary to understand the constitutional role of these two branches of government. The Supreme Court and the President operate within a system where powers and responsibilities are in practice shared by separate and distinct institutions. The Constitution groups national governmental functions under three general powers — legislative, executive and judicial — and provides for a co-ordinate status between the three institutions exercising these powers. Built into this formal separation of institutions is an elaborate pattern of checks and balances designed to make the activities of each partially but not wholly dependent on the actions and decisions of the others. Thus, for example, the nomination and appointment of Supreme Court Justices is initiated by the President, but the Senate must concur with the nomination. Justices are appointed for life, while the elected term of the President is fixed at four years with the possibility of re-election. Both may be removed from office if impeached by the House of Representatives for "treason, bribery, or other high crimes and misdemeanors", and found guilty by the Senate. If the President is impeached, the Chief Justice presides over the trial in the Senate.

What is striking in any examination of the rise and apparent demise of "the imperial Presidency" is how little of the authority claimed or assumed by recent Presidents was granted formally by the Constitution — as the centre page of the pamphlet reveals. This was a consequence of the suspicion of one-man executives inherited from the Revolution, and a practical recognition by the framers of the Constitution that the President must be given few specific powers in the Constitution itself if ratification of the document was to be obtained. Because the President was granted such a modest catalogue of powers, much of the development of executive authority has been assumed, or delegated by statute or by congressional resolution. More importantly for our purposes, it has required legitimization by decisions of the Supreme Court. To this extent presidential authority has often rested on shakier constitutional foundations than the more carefully defined powers of Congress. Presidents have been helped by the fact that they can initiate nominations to the Supreme Court, but this by no means guarantees that they can control in any systematic way the decisions of the Court. Hence analysis of the political interactions between the President and the Supreme Court provides an excellent illustration of how the Constitution, and the system of government which has evolved, operate in practice.

At the outset it was not clear what would be the precise role of the Supreme Court. However, there are strong grounds for suggesting that the Court was intended to be a check on the legislative branch, which the framers feared might pass laws popular with current majorities of the people but contrary to the intent of the Constitution. Robert Scigliano, in his study of relations between the Supreme Court and the Presidency,[4] argues that these two institutions were intended to act, in certain circumstances, as an informal alliance or check on the legislative authority of Congress, and have in fact done so. However valid this interpretation may be of the constitutional basis of the respective authority of these institutions, events have served to make the actual relationships between the three branches of the national government very different. While Congress has generally not fared as well as the President with respect to Supreme Court decisions, on occasions both the President and Congress have been allied against the Supreme Court. Relations between the President and the Supreme Court have not always been harmonious, as can be seen by brief reference to specific events before 1933.

A federal court structure was created by the Judiciary Act of 1789, but there was no conflict between a President and the Court until the appointment of John Marshall as Chief Justice.

The Federalists, heavily defeated in the 1800 elections, retreated into the judiciary. Marshall, formerly Secretary of State under President John Adams, became Chief Justice, and the lame-duck Federalist Congress created new federal judgeships to which Adams appointed worthy Federalists. The Federalists sought to 'pack' the judiciary as a possible check on the likely excesses of the new administration of Thomas Jefferson. Many Jeffersonians, however, believed that the judiciary had no right to control the popular will, which, as the source of the Constitution's authority, could by definition do nothing unconstitutional.

When the Jefferson administration refused to deliver a commission to William Marbury, a last-minute judicial appointee of Adams, the Supreme Court, acting on a petition by Marbury and others, issued a 'show cause' order to Secretary of State Madison regarding delivery of the signed commissions. Madison ignored the order, and the Court was faced with a direct challenge to its authority. If Marshall now decided that Marbury should be given his commission, the Jefferson administration would again ignore the Court, and there was no way in which the Court could enforce its decision.

Marshall, however, proved equal to the challenge. Speaking for the Court, he affirmed that Marbury had a legal right to the commission but that the Supreme Court could not issue a writ of mandamus to federal officials, as Marbury requested, because Section 13 of the 1789 Judiciary Act granting the Court this authority under original jurisdiction was unconstitutional. The Constitution clearly prescribed the original jurisdiction of the Supreme Court, Congress could not alter that jurisdiction, and its attempt to do so violated the Constitution.[5] As a legal opinion the decision was narrow and strained in its logic. However, for Marshall it achieved several purposes. It allowed him to lecture Madison and Jefferson on their constitutional obligations as executive officials. By deciding against Marbury he avoided the possibility of any defiance of a Court decision. Most significantly, in declaring part of a statute void because it gave the Court authority contrary to the Constitution, he established the principle that the Court could declare void an act of Congress, without risking charges that the Court was engaged in any self-aggrandizement of authority. By so acting he established implicitly, if not explicitly, that the Constitution incorporated the principle of judicial review — the power of the federal judiciary, especially the Supreme Court, to judge on the constitutionality of actions of the co-ordinate branches of the federal government, President as well as Congress, and if necessary to declare such actions unconstitutional.[6]

As the decision on the immediate issue did not seriously embarrass Jefferson, Marshall avoided a direct attack on the Court by Jefferson. However, the President soon showed his willingness to use impeachment as a means of controlling the judiciary. In a test case concerning the injudicious behaviour of Justice Chase, the Jeffersonian majority in the House initiated impeachment proceedings, but in the Senate the administration failed to secure the two-thirds majority necessary for conviction. Further conflict ensued during the treason trial of Aaron Burr, when Marshall subpoenaed Jefferson to appear before the Court with certain documents. Jefferson refused to obey the order, arguing that the independence of the executive would be jeopardized were the President to comply. In the trial itself Marshall excluded much of the government's testimony as irrelevant, and the jury found Burr not guilty. Though Jefferson contemplated the possible impeachment of Marshall at this time, he did not succeed in limiting the independence of the Supreme Court. In Scigliano's opinion, Jefferson, at least as President, "never openly acted or spoke against the judicial branch, or any decisions rendered by it, or openly expressed his view of the role of the judiciary in the system of separation of powers."[7]

Subsequently Marshall, who presided over the Court until 1835, made important assertions of national governmental authority in a series of decisions after 1815, and so affirmed the position and the duty of the Court as the final interpreter of the Constitution. Up to the Civil War, conflicts between Presidents and the Court occurred primarily over different interpretations of the role of the national government and of the judiciary within the national government, with Presidents such as Jackson often reflecting a states-rights or limited national-government position.

In the decades after the Civil War the legitimacy and authority of the Court seemed more firmly established than that of the President. Presidents were on the whole weak and did not associate themselves with clear-cut programmes of legislation. Hence they raised little objection when the Court began to strike down state and federal legislation deemed to infringe constitutional rights. Whereas Marshall had used judicial authority primarily to give substance to the constitutional powers of the national government, the Court now demonstrated that judicial review could be the vehicle for judicial "supremacy" of a different kind. Insisting on a narrow interpretation of the authority of the elected branches of government with respect to many social and economic matters, it did not hesitate to declare unconstitutional specific state and national laws.

By the early twentieth century, however, more energetic Presidents were coming to power who were sympathetic to social reforms and the regulation of business, and they began to express concern at the potential threat of judicial challenges to their policies. Theodore Roosevelt, while in office, confined himself to vigorous verbal questioning of the validity of the judiciary's claim to have the *final* say regarding constitutional interpretation, adding that appointed judges were incapable of formulating relevant legal precepts to meet contemporary problems. Woodrow Wilson also expressed concern about judicial "supremacy", but he in turn did not challenge directly the Court's authority. He did, however, come to recognize the potential significance of the President's power to initiate nominations to the Court. So indeed did conservatives like the former President, William Howard Taft, who by 1920 believed that control of judicial appointments was one of the major issues of the day. The Republican ascendancy of the following decade, however, ensured that Presidents would continue to respect, and by their judicial nominations reinforce, the conservative outlook of the Court on social and economic questions.

The use of judicial review by the Court in the Gilded Age and in the first third of the twentieth century was accepted in part because of public respect for its authority, but also because it was not out of step with dominant public attitudes of the time. [8] Furthermore, the Court did demonstrate that it could use its authority to expand the existing constitutional powers of the President in certain circumstances. For example, in the *Neagle* case of 1890 [9] the Court held that the Constitution's provision that the President shall "take care that the laws be faithfully executed" conferred an authority to protect all those who aid in the performance of federal governmental responsibilities. The Court found, in a clause that seemed to impose only a duty on the President, a grant of power to prevent violations of the peace of the United States. In 1895 this was extended when the Court ruled, in the *Debs* case,[10] that the President might use military force within a state to ensure that national instrumentalities such as the postal service could function properly. Similarly, in 1926 in the *Myers* case [11] the Court strengthened presidential control of executive-branch personnel by asserting that a President may remove a subordinate officer without seeking the consent of the Senate.

Hence up to 1933 Presidents rarely challenged judicial authority directly, and no clash seemed likely unless a popular President, willing to use his authority, was determined to implement reforms and changes of the sort the Supreme Court might consider to be unconstitutional. The conjunction of a grave political and economic emergency, an assertive and popular President, and a strong-willed judiciary, provided in 1933 the ingredients for a constitutional conflict of major dimensions.

2 : The New Deal and the Court, 1933-1938

The stock-market collapse of October 1929 precipitated the most serious economic depression in American history. In the face of this crisis, President Hoover was reluctant to recognize the need for major institutional changes or strong national governmental action.[12] Consequently the severity of the depression made economic issues dominant in the 1932 presidential election. The major challenge was to find policies which might restore economic stability and public confidence, alleviate economic inequalities, and avoid future depressions. Franklin D. Roosevelt gained the Democratic nomination, and in a series of campaign speeches captured the imagination and votes of many Americans by his powerful assertion of the need for bold experimentation and a "new deal" by government — which could be achieved only by strong executive leadership of the type evident before under Woodrow Wilson.

Elected to the Presidency along with large Democratic majorities in both houses of Congress, Roosevelt was given a mandate to use appropriate national authority to deal with the domestic crisis. In his inaugural address Roosevelt made it clear that he believed in a flexible interpretation of the Constitution and in the legitimacy of federal legislation to deal with the existing emergency. He promised to seek "broad Executive authority", and immediately sent a series of bills to Congress. In the famous Hundred Days, Congress passed an unprecedented amount of new legislation. The emergency programme initiated by Roosevelt constituted a far-reaching assertion of federal governmental authority over economic affairs and individuals alike, generally justified in terms of the general-welfare or the interstate-commerce clauses of the Constitution. Some of the legislation, moreover, contained substantial delegations of legislative authority to the executive. Those interests adversely affected by the new legislation speedily brought litigation, and it was evident that the attitude of the Supreme Court towards these measures would be of great importance.

The record of the Court suggested that it would not be sympathetic to the new initiatives. Through the 1920s the Court had been dominated by William Howard Taft, whom President Harding appointed Chief Justice in 1921. Under him the Court had declared unconstitutional state and federal laws relating to matters such as a minimum wage or the employment of children. Taft, retired in 1930, to be succeeded by the more moderate Charles Evan Hughes, but the personnel and outlook of the Court in 1933 had not changed greatly since the mid-twenties.

However, it was clear that the members of the Court would not find it easy to express a unanimous view on New Deal legislation. The most critical cases involved constitutional issues where Justices might produce equally relevant precedents to support either side of the argument. Four Justices (Van Devanter, Butler, McReynolds and Sutherland) had long-standing records of opposition to major extensions of federal governmental authority, especially with respect to the regulation of interstate commerce. Two Justices, Brandeis and Stone, seemed likely to be sympathetic to the extension of federal regulatory powers, though not necessarily of executive authority, and to the need for judicial restraint in order to permit the elected branches of government some flexibility in dealing with a crisis. Cardozo had been nominated somewhat reluctantly by Hoover in 1932 to meet the demands of a Democratic Senate, and he was expected to support Brandeis and Stone. Roberts had joined the Court in 1930, after Hoover's initial selection had been rejected by the Senate. He appealed to both conservatives and liberals in the Senate, and together with Hughes came to play a crucial role in the future events. The stage was set for a possible constitutional confrontation between the Court and the elected branches of government led by the President, but also for a constitutional debate within the Court itself, as Chief Justice Hughes unhappily recognized.

The Supreme Court did not consider a case involving a New Deal statute until January 1935, though in 1934 the validity of two state laws was sustained with a majority of the Justices accepting that controls might be necessary in emergencies if they were in the public interest. In the sixteen months that followed the Court considered ten cases, or groups of cases, involving the New Deal statutes. In eight instances the decisions went against Roosevelt and the New Deal agencies. Only two measures, one involving the Tennessee Valley Authority Act, were given guarded approval. Several of the invalidations were by unanimous or near-unanimous decisions, but some of the major ones were by the narrowest possible majority (5-4).

The first blow came in January 1935, in *Panama Refining Co. v. Ryan*.[13] The case concerned Section 9(c) of the National Industrial Recovery Act. This gave the President the authority to prohibit the transportation across state lines of oil produced in excess of limitations imposed by states in order to conserve resources and stabilize prices. There were precedents for such federal co-operation in the enforcement of state laws, but Hughes, speaking for eight of the nine Justices, declared that Section 9(c) was unconstitutional. He stated that it constituted an invalid delegation of legislative power because it set no guidelines or standards for executive action, nor any restrictions on executive discretion. Hence any executive orders issued under the authority of Section 9(c) were without constitutional authority. The Court thus, for the first time, held unconstitutional a provision in a statute delegating to the executive quasi-legislative authority.

In May 1935 the Court went further and in a unanimous opinion held the rest of the National Industrial Recovery Act to be unconstitutional. The Act had authorized a major industrial recovery programme co-ordinated by a National Recovery Administration. Through this the Roosevelt administration hoped to encourage the resumption of normal production, plus increased employment and wages. Codes of fair competition were set up which included certain provisions relating to the rights of workers. The Act had some initial beneficial effects, but by 1935 the NRA was in some disarray. The *Schechter* (or 'sick chicken') case[14] involved an appeal by slaughterhouse operators against a conviction for violation of the code of fair competition for the live-poultry industry in New York City. In his opinion Hughes considered three questions: was the law justified given the grave national crisis, did the law illegally delegate legislative power, and did it exceed the limits of the interstate commerce power? He answered the first question by asserting that extraordinary conditions did not "create or enlarge constitutional power", and assertions of extraconstitutional authority were precluded by the Tenth Amendment. To the second his answer was that the codes constituted a form of delegation utterly inconsistent with the constitutional duties of Congress. Finally, he affirmed that the poultry code attempted to regulate transactions *within* states and so exceeded the federal commerce power.

On the same day, in deciding the case of *Humphrey's Executor v. United States*,[15] the Court further embarrassed the President by declaring unanimously that his removal of a member of the

Federal Trade Commission was invalid. The Court held that Congress had conferred upon the Commission independence of the President, and so it was not an agent of the executive. This decision modified the *Myers* judgement of 1926, by holding that removal authority applied only to purely executive officers in the departments. Roosevelt was incensed by these decisions, seeing them as direct challenges to both his policies and his executive prerogatives. At a press conference he attacked the actions of the Court, but his dilemma was that here at least he was speaking out against a unanimous Court. His administration sought further legislation to regulate industry, and quietly began to consider ways of mounting a counter-attack against the Court.

On January 6th, 1936, the Supreme Court made its long-awaited decision on the second of the major New Deal recovery programmes. In *United States v. Butler*[16] the Court, dividing 6-3, ruled unconstitutional the processing tax of the Agricultural Adjustment Act. This decision revealed serious divisions within the Court with respect to certain constitutional issues raised by the New Deal legislation. Justice Roberts held the tax to be an illegitimate use of the taxing power. While Congress could tax and spend for the general welfare, it could not use the bait of tax revenue to effect federal regulation of economic activity such as agricultural production. Two other aspects of the case were significant. The first was the enunciation by Roberts of the role of the Justices in determining the constitutionality of legislation. His narrow, mechanistic approach and its consequences were challenged in a strong dissenting opinion by Justice Stone, supported by Brandeis and Cardozo, which not only attacked the logic of Roberts' opinion but the tendency of the Court to act as a super-legislature via tortured constructions of the Constitution. Stone's advocacy of judicial self-restraint, together with strong public criticism of the *Butler* decision, confirmed the views of some members of the Roosevelt administration that the real problem was not the Constitution but the composition of the Court. Hence a few Roosevelt appointments, now or if he were re-elected in 1936, could change the situation.

Moreover, there were several initiatives in Congress for legislation to restrict the Court's prerogative of judicial review, or to change the size of the Court. Any doubts as to the need to act were removed in May 1936 when the Court, again by a 6-3 vote, invalidated the Bituminous Coal Act of 1935,[17] and followed this up with a 5-4 decision setting aside a state minimum-wage law for women. In effect, in the words of Alpheus Thomas Mason, "From January through June, 1936, the Court wove a constitutional fabric so tight as to bind political power at all levels'',[18] a view shared by Roosevelt at the time. Nevertheless, putting first things first, Roosevelt concentrated on winning the 1936 Presidential election and gaining popular approval for the concrete achievements of the New Deal and his own style of executive leadership. In the Democratic platform and in his campaign he avoided specific statements as to what he might do regarding the Court, though opponents warned that a Roosevelt victory would lead to measures attacking the composition or the jurisdiction of the Court.

In November 1936 Roosevelt gained a landslide victory, winning the electoral-college votes of every state except Maine and Vermont. Very soon the Court would reconvene, and before it would be several cases challenging the validity of legislation initiated by Roosevelt. The options open to the President were several. He could wait for vacancies to occur, yet an unprecedented four years had gone by without such an opportunity. McReynolds and Sutherland, two of his strongest opponents, were elderly, but seemed determined to remain on the Court as long as he remained in the White House. He could wait and see whether the election result might lead one or two Justices to change their views. He could support various proposals to change the Court's power by legislation ór constitutional amendment, or recommend legislation to reorganize the judiciary. On February 5th, 1937, Roosevelt ended his silence by presenting legislation to Congress. There has been much speculation as to how and why Roosevelt acted in the way he did. Most interestingly, William Leuchtenburg[19] has argued that the President came to reject the view that the Court might change voluntarily, but believed that action through a constitutional amendment was difficult to frame and achieve quickly. He was unenthusiastic about various legislative proposals to change the jurisdiction of the Court, and finally agreed with Attorney General Cummings on the need for some plan to 'pack' the Court to permit the appointment of Justices in tune with the times. Cummings, in searching for an appropriate recommendation, came across one made in 1913 by Justice McReynolds, then Wilson's Attorney General! In essence McReynolds suggested that the President should be permitted to appoint additional federal judges for every judge in courts below the Supreme Court who failed to retire at the age of seventy. Cummings used this as the basis of a proposal which he put to Roosevelt relating the principles of age and additional appointments to reform of the entire judiciary. The scheme was attractive as there had been recent demands for more lower-court judges to relieve congestion, and complaints about the age of some of the Justices. Roosevelt accepted the proposal and a bill was drafted.

It was emphasized that the bill was intended to reorganize the federal judiciary rather than to 'pack' the Court. It provided that, whenever any federal judge who had served ten years or more failed to retire after reaching seventy, the President might appoint an additional judge to the court on which he served. No more than fifty additional judges might be appointed, and the maximum size of the Supreme Court was set at fifteen. In a message accompanying the bill, Roosevelt expressed his concern at the backlog of cases and for the efficiency of the federal courts in general. Most older judges were characterized as unable to perform their duties or antiquated in outlook.

Roosevelt had acted, but in an ultimately ineffective manner. It seemed obvious that the bill was a court-packing scheme in disguise. By failing to confront the real constitutional issue of the particular use of judicial review by the Court, it alienated his supporters on the Court and confused many of his congressional allies. Even Brandeis, himself eighty, joined Hughes in persuasively demolishing the charge that the Justices had a backlog of cases. Hughes wrote a letter to the Senate Judiciary Committee providing statistical evidence that no backlog existed and arguing that enlargement would impair the efficiency of the Court. This action undercut the validity of Roosevelt's proposal. The bill itself also weakened his political position, strengthening conservative opposition and creating a powerful public sentiment that his proposal was wrong in principle. In July the Senate rejected Roosevelt's bill, but as a gesture to the President later passed an uncontroversial Judiciary Reform Act.

Meanwhile the Court itself had removed the need for action. In a dramatic demonstration of an ability to recognize the force of public opinion and electoral realities, the Court, between March and June, validated state legislation and both the National Labour Relations and the Social Security Acts of 1935. Justice Van Devanter resigned, followed closely by Sutherland. The final victory appeared to be Roosevelt's. Between 1937 and 1943 he nominated a new Chief Justice and eight Associate Justices, and by 1942 the Court had accepted a substantial enlargement of national governmental authority over economic matters. In fact, the real situation was more fluid.

As Herman Pritchett has shown, the Justices appointed by Roosevelt were not united in their views.[20] If anything, they edged tentatively towards a new judicial role outlined initially by Justice Stone, a Republican appointee but Roosevelt's choice in 1941 as Chief Justice to succeed Hughes. In the otherwise obscure case of *United States v. Carolene Products Co.* in 1938,[21] Stone included in a footnote a practical guide for the application of the judicial self-restraint he had himself advocated in 1936 in his dissent from the *Butler* opinion. Put simply, his argument was

"Spring Practice" by Hungerford,
in the Pittsburgh Post Gazette, *April 1, 1937.*

that the Court should presume the constitutionality of economic legislation, deferring to the wishes of the elected branches of government, and confine the possible exercise of judicial activism to the defence of individual and minority rights as expressed in the Bill of Rights (the first ten amendments to the Constitution) and the Fourteenth Amendment.

The confrontation between Roosevelt and the Court had significant consequences for the authority of the President, but, above all it concerned the nature and spirit of the Constitution. In some respects it was a replay of the clash between Jefferson and Marshall. The major antagonists in both instances were the Chief Justice and the President. In neither instance was the Court's power formally under attack. Jefferson and Roosevelt, for different reasons, sought primarily to curb abuses of its authority but found Marshall and Hughes at least their equals in political skill. The failure of the court-packing plan and the judicial 'retreat' engineered by Hughes preserved the authority of the Court and meant that for a long time neither President nor Congress would try to curb the Court.

It can be argued that the conflict between Roosevelt and the Court was not over fundamental issues but about the specific use of authority by particular individuals. Roosevelt did not challenge the legitimacy of judicial review, only its particular use by the Hughes Court. In turn the Court did not challenge presidential power but up to 1937 questioned the delegation of certain authority to the President by Congress and the specific use of executive authority by a particular President. Hence both protagonists may be said to have shared a similar concern: that no single institution become too dominant, nor any set of office-holders so extreme in the use of their authority as to distort the purpose of the separation of powers. Roosevelt and others feared that the Court would become a "super-legislature", a group of non-elected Justices preventing the elected branches of government from implementing policies deemed to be in the national interest. The Court and its supporters feared the tyranny of the majority as reflected in a chief executive acting as a virtual dictator in domestic affairs in certain circumstances. In fact both institutions emerged scarred but essentially unscathed, able in turn to have a significant influence on public policy, and sufficiently powerful for charges of "executive dictatorship" and "government by judiciary" to be made again in the future.

3: Foreign Affairs and National Emergencies, 1936-1952

Relations between the President and the Supreme Court in the 1930s demonstrate that the Court was prepared to challenge any extensions of executive authority to deal with domestic 'emergencies', whether such authority was claimed by a particular President or delegated to the executive by Congress. With respect to foreign affairs, the general attitude of the Court has been different. While the Constitution divides the power over foreign affairs between the President and the Senate, and invites a degree of conflict over the privilege of making foreign policy, the President has certain advantages. Unlike domestic affairs, foreign policy has been deemed to be inherently a national governmental responsibility and an area in which the executive has particular responsibilities and obligations to respond to international crises and, in times of war, to use his authority as commander-in-chief of the armed forces.

The political and constitutional problems raised by World War II and America's new international position in the era of the Cold War were massive but not unprecedented. Roosevelt's conduct in the international crisis between 1939 and 1941 was analogous constitutionally to that of Lincoln in the Civil War crisis, and provides an important illustration of the dilemma that may face the Court when a President is forced in time of war or threat to national security to assume prerogative powers hitherto considered neither necessary nor constitutional. At the time of the Civil War certain issues arose concerning the nature of war powers (Congress having the authority to declare war), and important precedents were set by the Supreme Court. Overall, the Court showed restraint. In the *Prize Cases* in 1863[22] a majority of the Court upheld the legality of the President's decision to order the capture of certain neutral ships and cargoes. Their opinion stated that while the President could not initiate war, when it was begun by insurrection he must accept responsibility without waiting for legislative authority and "must determine what degree of force the crisis demands." A minority of four Justices insisted that the basic war power belonged to Congress. The same issue was raised during World War I, but most of the critical war measures never came before the Court, and with one exception the few that did came well after the Armistice. As in the Civil War, the Court found it difficult to challenge the constitutionality of a federal war activity while the war was in progress. Moreover, war was formally declared by Congress and Wilson acted from the beginning through broad grants of authority delegated to him by Congress.

Roosevelt's ability to take initiatives in the face of the various threats to national security between 1939 and 1941 was helped considerably by a decision of the Court in 1936,[23] written by Justice Sutherland, at that time the *bête noire* of the New Dealers. In 1934 Congress had passed a joint resolution permitting the President to place embargoes on the sale of arms and ammunition to warring nations. The resolution placed no restriction on the President's discretion in establishing such embargoes. Roosevelt declared an embargo on the sale of arms and munitions to Bolivia and Paraguay, and the Curtiss-Wright Export Corporation was indicted for selling arms to Bolivia. Curtiss-Wright claimed that the embargo was an unconstitutional delegation of legislative power, an argument the Court had found persuasive in recent cases relating to New Deal economic programmes.

The Supreme Court rejected this argument. Justice Sutherland stated that the rule regarding delegation of power was a restriction on Congress in domestic affairs, but was irrelevant in foreign affairs, because here the national government had certain inherent powers. As to who should exercise these powers, Sutherland came close to holding that these rested almost exclusively with the President. Hence it was not necessary to demonstrate the validity of the joint resolution, since Roosevelt might have established an embargo on his own initiative. Sutherland's view that the President is the "sole organ" of the federal government in foreign relations seemed to make him the sole executor of American foreign policy, even if such authority "must be exercised in subordination to the applicable provisions of the Constitution."

This was an important concession to executive authority which Roosevelt exploited both before and during World War II, without any direct challenge from the Court.[24] While it is conceivable that Roosevelt's continued use of executive prerogatives in foreign policy and of his powers as commander-in-chief without a formal declaration of war might have provoked a constitutional crisis, this became academic after the attack on Pearl Harbor in December 1941.

The question of the civil liberties and legal rights of citizens in times of war or times of international crisis has posed a more delicate issue for the Supreme Court. Lincoln's suspension of the privilege of the writ of habeas corpus led Chief Justice Taney in *Ex parte Merryman* (1861)[25] to deny the right of the President so to act, arguing that only an act of Congress could effect this and concluding that if this action were permitted the people would no longer be living under "a government of laws". Lincoln responded by arguing that the Constitution was silent as to who may suspend habeas corpus in an emergency, and continued to enforce it until Congress acted two years later. Following World War I, the Court upheld the constitutionality of the 1917 Espionage Act and the 1918 Sedition Act, which empowered the executive branch to punish expressions of opinion hostile to the government.

During and immediately after World War II the Court, dominated by Roosevelt appointees, demonstrated that the guideline provided by Stone regarding judicial intervention was unlikely to be applied in times of war, or even in the uncertain era of the Cold War, to protect the rights of individual citizens or groups of citizens against national governmental actions deemed necessary to maintain national security. For example, during the war the Court sustained an executive order, based on the commander-in-chief powers and later supported by statute, authorizing the Secretary of War to prescribe certain military areas from which persons might be excluded. This led to the segregation and internment in relocation camps of many thousands of Japanese-Americans, many of them citizens. Although given three opportunities in 1943-44, the Court never directly considered the legality of this action, nor the issue of the government's authority to restrict the rights of American citizens when required by military necessity. In the *Hirabayashi* case the Court upheld a military curfew order, and in the *Korematsu* case upheld the exclusion programme without discussing the detention aspect, though three Justices vigorously dissented. Only in *Ex parte Endo* did the Court indicate concern, suggesting that the authorities should not detain citizens who had demonstrated their undoubted loyalty.[26]

Furthermore, in the years that followed, the Court, led after 1946 by the Truman appointee Fred Vinson, did not challenge the dominant political attitudes of the early Cold War years regarding internal security. For example, in *Dennis v. United States* (1951)[27] the Court sustained the constitutionality of the 1940 Smith Act, which had forbidden conspiracies to teach or advocate the violent overthrow of the government. Technically known as the Alien Registration Act, this law had been intended as a war measure comparable to the 1918 Sedition Act, but had been used in peace-time by the Truman administration to prosecute leading Communists.

However, the most significant event in relations between the Court and the President in this period arose when a domestic crisis in industrial relations coincided with an international emergency. In 1950 President Truman committed American troops to the defence of South Korea against a North Korean invasion. Congress did not formally declare war, even though the military action undertaken on the President's authority dragged on for three years. At the end of 1951 a dispute in the steel industry led to a threat of strike action which the executive felt might have severe repercussions on the military effort in Korea. Efforts to obtain a compromise through the Wage Stabilization Board failed, and the steelworkers' union called for a nation-wide strike.

The President could have resorted to the Taft-Hartley Act which, among other things, permitted the President to obtain an injunction postponing for eighty days any strike threatening the national welfare. This act had been passed in 1947 by a Congress which had become controlled by the Republicans in 1946 for the first time since the Hoover presidency. The legislation reflected their view that a series of major strikes after the end of the war had shown that the labour unions had become too powerful, and that there was a need to equalize the positions of labour and management *vis-à-vis* government. The unions, however, felt that the legislation severely restricted their activities. The President, whose good relations with organized labour had been damaged by his firm action during the strikes in 1946, seized the opportunity to veto the bill. When Congress overrode the veto, Truman used the issue to obtain labour support in his narrowly successful re-election bid in 1948. In the steel dispute in 1951 he was understandably reluctant to use the Taft-Hartley procedure, especially as he believed that the companies rather than the unions were the main obstacle to a settlement.

On the eve of the strike the President issued an executive order instructing Secretary of Commerce Sawyer to take over operation of the steel mills for the United States government. Addressing the nation, Truman declared that the country faced a serious emergency, that its security depended upon steel as a major component of defence production, and that the Taft-Hartley procedure would have meant at least a short interruption in production. The President based his authority for acting on his powers as commander-in-chief of the armed forces and on inherent powers derived from the aggregate of powers granted to the President by the Constitution. He reported the seizure to Congress in a special message in which he invited them to legislate on the subject.

The immediate response was not unfavourable, though there was some press and congressional criticism. The steel companies were angry, and responded with attempts both to influence public opinion and to bring legal action against the President. Attention was quickly diverted from the facts of the case to the high-handed decision of the President. Truman went out of his way to stress that he had acted in terms of the inherent powers of the executive under the Constitution, which obliged him, in an emergency, to take whatever action he deemed necessary to protect the national interest.

Truman's argument did not commend itself to the district court when the steel companies filed for an injunction against the seizure, but the court of appeals accepted a government request to stay such an injunction and allow the Supreme Court to consider the case. The steel companies took the initiative, and the case was argued before the Court. Two weeks later the Court gave its ruling in *Youngstown Sheet and Tube Co. v. Sawyer.*[28] Truman expected his action to be upheld, and few people believed that a Court composed of five Roosevelt and four Truman appointees would call a halt to the accretion of executive power. Writings by distinguished scholars at the time also supported the view that presidential authority, especially with respect to emergency situations, had been irrevocably expanded and that the Supreme Court was unlikely to interfere with its development or with conflicts between the executive branch and Congress.[29]

Having agreed to consider the case, there were several ways in which it might have been decided. For example, the case could have been dismissed because it involved a "political question" which could be dealt with only by the elected branches of government. Instead, by a 6-3 vote the Court held that the seizure by the President was an unconstitutional usurpation of legislative power. The decision, however, was less clear-cut than the figures suggest. Although a majority opinion was written by Justice Black, every other Justice in the majority insisted on writing a separate concurring opinion, and one refused to join in the Court's opinion concurring only in the result.[30] Seven opinions were written in all. As a result, the decision did not have the same impact as a single, agreed, majority or unanimous verdict.

The result, according to Schlesinger, was "a confusing, if intermittently dazzling, examination of the presidential claim to emergency prerogative."[31] Justice Black addressed the issue of presidential power directly, asserting that it must originate from an act of Congress or from the Constitution. No act of Congress authorized Truman's seizure, therefore the power had to come from the Constitution. He rejected the contention of the executive that the seizure power could be implied from the aggregate of powers granted to the President by the Constitution. It could not be justified as an application of the President's military power as commander-in-chief, nor from his general executive powers, which do not include lawmaking. Black interpreted the separation-of-powers doctrine rigidly, a view shared by Justice Douglas. Both agreed that the seizure was a legislative power exercisable by the executive only with congressional authorization. The four other majority Justices rejected this formal position. Justice Frankfurter adopted a flexible approach, related to the specific issues. He argued that in 1947 Congress had deliberately not included seizure authority in the Taft-Hartley Act, and in seizing the steel plants Truman had exceeded his responsibility to execute the laws faithfully. He reiterated the view of Brandeis and others that the principle of the separation of powers was adopted in 1787 in order to preclude the exercise of arbitrary power.

The concurring opinion of Justice Jackson emphasized that practical realities left a "twilight zone" where Congress and the President might act together, or where actual authority was unclear. The legitimacy of unilateral executive action could only be justified if it was clear that Congress could not act. Such was not the case here. Jackson refuted the executive's claim that all inherent powers rested with the President, attacked the use of the limited war powers granted to the President "as an instrument of domestic policy", and rejected the use of inherent powers without statutory support. He pointed out that, in a similar crisis situation, Roosevelt had based his New Deal authority on delegated congressional, not inherent presidential, power. Thus the four Justices — Black, Douglas, Frankfurter and Jackson — who had been fervent supporters of the New Deal did not see it as a precedent for the steel seizure. Justices Burton and Clarke also could not regard the emergency as grave enough to warrant Truman's action, but did not rule out the possibility that emergencies might occur in which a President could act even if Congress had not prescribed procedures for such action. Here, however, Congress had done so.

Interestingly, Chief Justice Vinson, a close political and personal friend of President Truman, wrote a strong dissenting opinion. Supported by Justices Reed and Minton, he defended the action taken by Truman. He argued that the President had acted wholly in accordance with his obligations under the Constitution. Citing the decisions of the Court in the *Neagle* and *Debs* cases, he deemed the emergency to be of the kind that, if the President had any constitutional authority to act in any situation without congressional direction, the seizure was warranted.

On its face the decision suggested that the Supreme Court had repudiated any claims for an inherent executive prerogative in internal affairs, or any expanded prerogatives in national emergen-

be eligible to that office, who shall not have attained to the age of thirty-five years, and been fourteen years a resident within the United States.

VI. In case of the removal of the President from office, or of his death, resignation, or inability to discharge the powers and duties of the said office, the same shall devolve on the Vice-president; and the Congress may by law provide for the case of removal, death, resignation, or inability, both of the President and Vice-president, declaring what officer shall then act as President: and such officer shall act accordingly, until the disability be removed, or a President shall be elected.

VII. The President shall, at stated times, receive for his services a compensation, which shall neither be increased nor diminished during the period for which he shall have been elected: and he shall not receive, within that period, any other emolument from the United States, or any of them.

VIII. Before he enters on the execution of his office, he shall take the following oath or affirmation:

"I do solemnly swear (or affirm) that I will faithfully execute the office of President of the United States; and will, to the best of my ability, preserve, protect, and defend the Constitution of the United States."

SECTION II.

I. The President shall be Commander in Chief of the army and navy of the United States, and of the militia of the several States, when called into the actual service of the United States. He may require the opinion in writing of the principal officers in each of the executive departments, upon any subject relating to the duties of their respective offices: and he shall have power to grant reprieves and pardons for offences against the United States, except in cases of impeachment.

II. He shall have power, by and with the advice and consent of the Senate, to make treaties, provided two thirds of the Senators present concur: and he shall nominate, and by and with the advice and consent of the Senate shall appoint ambassadors, other public Ministers and Consuls, Judges of the Supreme Court, and all other officers of the United States, whose appointments are not herein otherwise provided for, and which shall be established by law. But the Congress may by law vest the appointment of such inferior officers as they think proper, in the President alone, in the courts of law, or in the heads of departments.

SECTION III.

III. The President shall have power to fill up all vacancies that may happen during the recess of the Senate, by granting commissions, which shall expire at the end of their next session.

He shall from time to time give to the Congress information of the state of the Union; and recommend to their consideration such measures as he shall judge necessary and expedient. He may, on extraor-

extraordinary occasions, convene both Houses, or either of them and in case of disagreement between them, with respect to the time of adjournment, he may adjourn them to such time as he shall think proper. He shall receive ambassadors and other public ministers. He shall take care that the laws be faithfully executed, and shall commission all the officers of the United States.

SECTION IV.

The President, Vice-president, and all civil officers of the United States, shall be removed from office, on impeachment for, and conviction of treason, bribery, or other high crimes and misdemeanors.

ARTICLE III. SECTION I.

The judicial power of the United States shall be vested in one Supreme Court, and in such inferior courts as the Congress may, from time to time, ordain and establish. The Judges, both of the Supreme and inferior Courts, shall hold their offices during good behaviour; and shall, at stated times, receive for their services, a compensation, which shall not be diminished during their continuance in office.

SECTION II.

The judicial power shall extend to all cases in law and equity arising under this Constitution, the laws of the United States, and treaties made, or which shall be made under their authority; to all cases affecting Ambassadors, other public Ministers and Consuls; to all cases of admiralty and maritime jurisdiction; to controversies to which the United States shall be a party; to controversies between two or more States; between a State and citizens of another State; between citizens of different States; between citizens of the same State, claiming lands under grants of different States; and between a State, or the citizens thereof, and foreign States, citizens, or subjects.

II. In all cases affecting Ambassadors, other public Ministers and Consuls, and those in which a State shall be a party, the Supreme Court shall have original jurisdiction. In all the other cases before mentioned, the Supreme Court shall have appellate jurisdiction both as to law and fact, with such exceptions, and under such regulations, as the Congress shall make.

III. The trial of all crimes, except in cases of impeachment, shall be by jury; and such trial shall be held in the State where the said crimes shall have been committed; but when not committed within any State, the trial shall be at such place or places as the Congress may by law have directed.

SECTION III.

I. Treason against the United States shall consist only in levying war against them, or in adhering to their enemies, giving them aid and comfort. No person shall be convicted of treason unless on the testimony of two witnesses to the same overt act, or on confession in open court.

II. The Congress shall have power to declare the punishment of

The United States Constitution, in the first section of Article II, declares that "The executive power shall be vested in a President of the United States of America", and then prescribes procedures for his election as well as determining other details. The second and third sections define his powers, while Article III is devoted to "the judicial power". The text above is reproduced from William Cobbett, Porcupine's Works . . . Exhibiting A Faithful Picture of the United States of America *(London, 1801), vol. 1.*

cies. Yet the decision as a whole did not exclude presidential initiative in an indisputable crisis, but did draw attention to the importance of Congress in providing procedures whereby Presidents might take emergency action. If the Court did not deny totally the recourse to emergency powers, it did challenge the growing mystique of executive authority and autonomy. The decision also was greeted favourably by Congress and by public opinion, despite the fact that a steel strike was impending.[32]

In retrospect the decision seems little more than a minor hiccup in the accumulation of executive authority. It had a marginal bearing on unilateral presidential action in foreign affairs. Yet the Court, without abandoning the principle of self-restraint, made it clear that presidential actions were not immune from judicial review, even after the New Deal 'revolution'.

4: The Warren Court, Civil Rights, and the Nixon Response

In 1952 General Eisenhower was elected President as a Republican. In domestic affairs it soon became apparent that he did not wish to provide leadership, preferring to defer to the legislative process. In September 1953, eight months after Eisenhower assumed office, Chief Justice Vinson died. Eisenhower gave careful consideration to the task of making his first Court nomination, and finally decided on Governor Earl Warren of California. There were sound practical, legal and political reasons for his choice. Warren had been influential in helping Eisenhower obtain the Republican nomination. He possessed the leadership qualities and administrative skills to be Chief Justice. He had some legal experience and an impressive political record. The nature of the latter was raised by several conservative Senators at the confirmation hearings, where he was unfairly charged with having "left-wing", ultra-liberal views.

Almost immediately after his appointment was approved he became a controversial figure. On May 17th, 1954, speaking for a unanimous Court, Warren delivered the bombshell decision in *Brown v. Board of Education of Topeka*.[33] He declared that racial segregation in public education was inherently discriminatory and in violation of the "equal protection of the laws" clause of the Fourteenth Amendment. This dramatic decision, in effect, reversed the 1896 Court decision[34] which had upheld the right of state governments to distinguish between their citizens on the basis of race. The effect of this decision had been to make the principle of "separate but equal" the legal rationale in the Southern states for the segregation of whites and blacks in all kinds of public and private facilities.

Warren relied heavily on sociological and psychological evidence to support the view that separate educational facilities are inherently unequal. The basic constitutional issue was whether enforced racial segregation, even if all other factors might be equal, deprived the minority group of equal educational opportunity. The nine Justices seemed agreed that it did.

Because the decision seemed certain to provoke bitter controversy and problems of implementation for the lower courts, the Court later ruled that the transition from segregation to desegregation should take place "with all deliberate speed". Though it prompted a public furor, especially in the South, the decision was in fact the culmination of a line of policy and precedent developed since 1938 by the Court, and was made only after a series of conferences by the Justices which had begun before Warren became Chief Justice. However, if it was not a revolutionary doctrine, it *was* a classic example of judicial policy-making, and it marked the beginning of a new style of adjudication by the Court.[35] The Warren Court initiated a policy which Congress, under existing Senate rules and given the dominant influence of Southern Democratic Senators, would not support. It also provided the impetus for black groups who had sponsored the case to create the civil rights movement.[36]

The decision highlights the strengths and weaknesses of the Court. For some it was evidence of judicial statesmanship, while others attacked the Court for usurping the powers of the political branches of government. In point of fact, for almost a decade there was much deliberation but very little speed, and little help was forthcoming from the Eisenhower administration. Ingenious devices were employed by state governments and local school boards in the South to avoid compliance, and litigation in the courts posed serious dilemmas for Southern federal judges obliged to take note of the decision.[37] Eisenhower refused to state whether he agreed with the *Brown* decision, and only when there was violent resistance in 1957 to school desegregation in Little Rock, Arkansas, did he support the authority and supremacy of the federal courts. His action in placing the National Guard under federal authority and sending in troops to ensure peaceful integration was as much a response to the recalcitrance of Governor Faubus as evidence of an executive commitment to aid efforts at desegregation. In 1957 and 1960 Congress passed modest civil rights bills but Eisenhower gave only lukewarm support on both occasions, especially towards efforts to permit legal action by the Department of Justice to seek enforcement of school desegregation. In 1958 and again in 1964 the Court expressed disquiet at the slow pace of compliance with the *Brown* decision.[38]

Initiatives to speed desegregation through executive action were increased after the election of President Kennedy. Kennedy made a moral and practical commitment to civil rights, but efforts to obtain far-reaching legislation faced serious opposition in Congress from Southern Representatives and Senators. Not until crises occurred over the admission of black students to state universities in Alabama and Mississippi which involved the further use of federal troops did Kennedy move to initiate civil rights legislation in Congress. Only after the assassination of Kennedy did the executive, through the legislative skills of President Johnson, persuade Congress to accept the need for comprehensive action. There followed the Civil Rights Acts of 1964 and 1968, and the 1965 Voting Rights Act.

Beginning with the *Brown* decision, the Court led by Warren sought for over a decade to eradicate public and private racial discrimination. Acting alone, the Court was largely unsuccessful. A government-department study in 1968 revealed that over 60 per cent of black and white students still attended largely segregated schools. The major developments towards racial justice came belatedly, as a result of action by Congress and the President. Yet it is plausible to argue that little of this would have taken place without the Court initiative of 1954. In this sense the Court forced the elected branches of government to recognize the validity of the claims of significant minorities of Americans to equal protection and guarantee of their rights as citizens. On this, and later on other issues such as legislative reapportionment or equal voting rights,[39] the Warren Court was prepared to respond to perceived injustices in the absence of executive or congressional action. The Court also made a series of controversial decisions defending the rights of individuals in terms of the Bill of Rights, as, for example, when it restricted the operation of the 1940 Smith Act and declared unconstitutional several other measures used to penalize American Communists.[40] Such actions antagonized many interests in society and prompted demands in the 1960s for the impeachment of Warren.

The almost obsessive concern of the Warren Court with the importance of equality under and before the law in American society, whether with respect to voting rights, education, or the rights of criminal defendants, led the Court into a situation not unlike that in the early 1930s. Having ventured into the "political thicket", it soon had to decide complex matters of detail which are ideally determined best by the legislature. Moreover, the Court not only began to assume unusual authority for itself but showed little confidence in, or respect for, the legislative process. In contrast to the 1930s, however, the Presidency was little affected by this arrogation of power by the judiciary. Indeed the Warren Court was only mildly restrictive of the executive, and in general contributed to the expansion of the authority of the modern President. Relations remained cordial in the Kennedy and Johnson administrations, as the Court was often making decisions which had the general support of these administrations. This is not too surprising since the new era of judicial activism was more than just the erratic application of the "preferred position" doctrine initiated by Stone. In essence it was, as Martin Shapiro has indicated, "the history of a political institution working out the implications of the victory of the New Deal coalition and the dominance of the New Deal consensus."[41] Hence, while the attacks made on the decisions of the Warren Court echoed those made in the 1930s, they came from members of Congress rather than from the White House.[42] President Johnson on one occasion referred to Warren as the greatest Chief Justice of all time, and, as Roosevelt had with Justice Frankfurter, so Johnson sought advice and guidance from Justice Fortas.

Up until 1968 the judicial activism of the Warren Court was by and large on behalf of the current 'winners' in national politics. By 1968, as Richard Funston and others have argued, both the President and the Court had become out of step with the attitudes of many Americans.[43] The Court's lack of public support and prestige at this time was reflected in the Gallup Polls. The Democratic presidential defeat in 1968 was the result not only of reactions against the Vietnam policy of President Johnson abroad and the mixed blessings of his Great Society legislation at home, but also of the defection of Southern Democrats to support Governor Wallace of Alabama, the new symbol of Southern opposition to *Brown* and other Court decisions.

Opposition also expressed itself in the struggle to appoint a successor to Warren. In June 1968 the Chief Justice informed Johnson of his desire to retire, and the President duly nominated his *confidant* Fortas, who was also a member of the egalitarian majority on the Court. The Senate, reacting to charges of "cronyism" and questionable extrajudicial activities by the nominee, refused to confirm him. This action may be seen as indicating a loss of credibility for the Warren Court similar to that which had already forced Johnson not to seek renomination by his party in 1968. Fortas was simply an inappropriate choice for Chief Justice by a lame-duck President. The conflict did not end here, for new revelations of doubtful extrajudicial activities led Fortas to resign from the Court in 1969.

Chief Justice Warren withdrew his resignation, and remained on the Court until May 1969. The Fortas debacle was an important reminder of the significance of Supreme Court nominations, and a stimulus to the Senate to use its power to confirm nominations as part of a wider campaign to reassert congressional checks on the executive. The Republicans won the Presidency in 1968, but the Democrats retained control of the House and Senate. The political situation was therefore ripe for conflict between the President and Congress, with the Court as a central issue.

No President since Franklin Roosevelt had made the Supreme Court a major election issue, or raised public expectations that he could and would change the nature and style of judicial decisions, as Richard Nixon did in 1968. In campaign speeches Nixon asserted the need for a Court and a judicial system which looked upon its function as that of interpreting existing laws rather than taking initiatives. He promised to "rebalance" the Court with "strict constructionists", a label which was politically useful at the time but difficult to define precisely. While Nixon's notion of "strict construction" was little more than an indirect denunciation of the Warren Court, it struck a responsive chord among voters, especially in the South. Nixon himself hoped for a more subdued Court, one that would go about its constitutional activities with caution and deference to the other branches of government, leaving major national policy decisions to elected politicians, not least to the President.

President Nixon's first nominee, Warren Burger, was accepted by the Senate following the resignation of Chief Justice Warren. However, Nixon's undisguised views about the Court led to trouble over his next nominee. In August 1969 Nixon nominated Clement F. Haynsworth, Jr., to fill the position vacated by Fortas. Haynsworth was a Southerner and chief judge of a federal Circuit Court of Appeals. After the Burger appointment, Nixon had been urged to name a Southerner to the Court as final confirmation of his identification with Southern attitudes which had aided his election. Civil rights and labour leaders immediately voiced opposition, but more serious was evidence produced at the Senate hearings on the nomination that Haynsworth had participated in decisions indirectly affecting the welfare of companies in which

U. S. Capitol, January 20, 1969

A MOMENT OF IRONY? Chief Justice Earl Warren congratulates Richard Nixon who has just taken the oath of office for the first time. Mrs. Nixon holds the two Milhous family bibles upon which the oath was taken. The retiring President, Lyndon Johnson, leads the applause.

he had a monetary interest. Opponents of the nomination seized on this evidence, but ultimately it was the reaction of Nixon himself which brought about the rejection of Haynsworth. In the face of demands to withdraw the nomination Nixon became defensive and political. Rather than stressing the competence and the judicial record of his nominee, Nixon chose to reassert his desire to appoint a "conservative", and put strong and direct pressure on Republican Senators to support him. In the end it was the defections of liberal Republicans and the three top Republican leaders in the Senate that proved critical in denying confirmation. Nixon expressed bitter regret at the decision, but vowed to nominate another candidate with the same "legal philosophy" as Haynsworth.

In January 1970 he nominated G. Harrold Carswell of Florida, another Southern Appeal Court judge. It seemed unlikely that Republicans would go against their President a second time, especially as there was now no evidence of any ethical improprieties or conflict of interests. However, the situation changed dramatically when the news media disclosed that in 1948 Carswell had made a speech supporting segregation and white supremacy. Carswell immediately repudiated any continuing belief in such ideas, but closer scrutiny of his record revealed damaging evidence of racist actions both personal and on the bench. This, allied to growing criticism from within the legal profession as to his competence as a jurist, strengthened opposition to the nomination.

Once again the President attacked the Senate, asserting that its "advice and consent" authority was a passive constitutional function. Rejection would impair the constitutional relationship of the President to Congress. He argued that the central issue in the nomination was whether his constitutional responsibility to appoint members of the Court could be frustrated by those who would substitute their own philosophy or subjective judgement. He believed that he was not being accorded the same right of choice as that given to previous Presidents. Nixon's argument was a weak one, not least in that the Senate had in fact countermanded the choice of the President on twenty-four occasions before it rejected Carswell, often at times of intense political conflict between Presidents and the Senate. It had no foundation either in terms of the intentions of the framers of the Constitution or past practice, and was a deliberate attempt to transform his nominating authority into an exclusive appointing power. It strengthened the resolve of certain Senators to oppose the Carswell nomination, and thirteen Republicans voted against the nomination, which was duly rejected in April. Nixon asserted that the real reason for these rejections remained the fact that his nominees were strict constructionists and Southerners, and vowed that until the Senate was changed he would not nominate another Southerner. Within a week he named Harry A. Blackmun of Minnesota to fill the vacant Court seat. On May 12th the Senate approved the nomination by a 94-0 vote. In 1971 Nixon nominated and obtained the appointment of two other Justices, one (Powell) from Virginia.

The conflict between Nixon and the Senate over the two nominations is significant in demonstrating the importance that President Nixon attached to the need to obtain a Court dominated by Justices with attitudes very different from those which were predominant in the Warren era, and the extent to which he was prepared to claim total executive authority in order to get his nominees accepted. He failed in his latter efforts, though they did serve to consolidate his political support in the South.

In fact, in his first term as President, Nixon nominated more members of the Court in a four-year period than any President since Harding. Also, between 1969 and 1976 Congress approved over a dozen measures which had a direct impact on the functioning of the federal judiciary. They included an increase in the number of federal judges, so that by early in his second term Nixon had appointed more federal judges than any other President, most of them Republican loyalists who shared his belief in total judicial restraint. Despite these changes the results did not match Nixon's expectations.[44]

While the Supreme Court led by Burger, containing four Nixon appointees, came to behave in ways different from those of the Warren Court, there was no fundamental shift of attitude on the sensitive issue of civil rights. In 1969 Burger wrote a short opinion for a unanimous Court demanding the immediate termination of dual school systems, thus undercutting the efforts of the Nixon administration to encourage a 'go-slow' on desegregation; and in 1971 he wrote the majority opinion sustaining the use of busing to eliminate school segregation.[45] Even concerning issues such as law and order or criminal-law procedures, the change was one of degree or emphasis. The decisions of the majority of Justices on race relations, reapportionment, or the rights of criminal defendants constituted neither a new pattern of decision-making nor the erasure of the Warren legacy. Just as Eisenhower's appointment of Warren had not halted certain trends in Court decisions, so Nixon as President failed to 'reform' the Court.

Indeed, the Nixon appointees tended to display a judicial attitude more potent and conservative than the "strict constructionist" rhetoric of Nixon: for they recognized the importance of deferring to established precedents and upholding the legitimacy of the judicial and constitutional processes. Ironically, it was Nixon's own inability or unwillingness to recognize that the President also might be prudent to observe the constitutional limits on his authority that ultimately destroyed his Presidency.

5: The Court and the Revolutionary Presidency

The origins of the crisis which ended with the resignation of President Nixon lay in the emergence not of an imperious judiciary, but of the imperial Presidency. The latter was essentially the consequence of the complexities of international affairs which produced an unprecedented centralization of decisions over war and peace in the Presidency, and the unprecedented exclusion of others from policy-making. The Vietnam war accelerated this pattern of centralization and exclusion. Arthur Schlesinger, Jr., in explaining these developments, clearly indicates how in the 1960s and early 1970s there emerged an equivalent centralization of power in the domestic political process. Executive claims to inherent and exclusive authority, already triumphant in foreign affairs, now began to be made over domestic matters.[46]

In effect, Nixon began to establish a 'revolutionary' or 'plebiscitary' Presidency in both foreign and domestic affairs. Schlesinger has outlined the remarkable range of Nixon innovations up to 1972 — his appropriation of the war-making power, his particular interpretation of the appointing power, his unilateral efforts to abolish existing statutory programmes, his enlargement of executive privilege, his theories of impoundment and pocket veto — which together constituted "a new balance of constitutional powers".[47] Congress rallied to challenge and contest such developments and belatedly to reassert its own constitutional authority, but the 1972 landslide election victory of Nixon seemed to be a vindication of his position.

The Supreme Court did little to halt the growth of the imperial Presidency. It refused to give an opinion on whether the President could constitutionally commit American troops to protracted action in South-East Asia without a congressional declaration of war. In 1968 it rejected a petition regarding the legality of the American involvement in Vietnam, though Justice Douglas wrote a lengthy dissenting opinion arguing that the Court should answer the question whether conscription was constitutional in the absence of a declaration of war. In November 1970 the Court refused to allow the state of Massachusetts to file a suit against the Vietnam War. Again Justice Douglas wrote a dissenting opinion, and was supported by two other Justices.[48] However, in 1971 the Court did give a brief opinion, supported by six Justices, permitting the publication of the so-called Pentagon Papers, and rejecting the arguments of the Nixon administration. The Papers revealed the strategic planning of the Vietnam involvement by the Johnson administration, and their publication dramatized the whole issue of national security and secrecy with respect to information on foreign policy, and of executive prerogatives in this area.[49] The administration was unhappy at this failure to obtain judicial support for its claim of inherent power to protect national security. The Court also gave modest protection to anti-Vietnam War protesters. Nevertheless, if the Court had not fulfilled Nixon's expectations, up to 1972 it did not seriously embarrass him. Subsequently, however, the courts as a whole rendered verdicts which reflected unease with the claims and attitudes of the Nixon administration.

The 1972 election victory was followed immediately by a series of domestic initiatives by the Nixon administration. Among them were several executive orders demanding that certain funds appropriated by Congress, in particular for antipoverty programmes and environmental protection, should not be spent by the agencies concerned. This was a major escalation of executive impoundment of funds appropriated by Congress for programmes which the Nixon administration did not like. There were precedents for such actions, but their scale and character were a direct challenge to the clear power of the purse granted to Congress by the Constitution. When linked with the earlier refusal to enforce Title VI of the 1964 Civil Rights Act (which required that federal money be withheld from programmes or organizations that discriminated racially) and with Nixon's use of the pocket veto when Congress was only temporarily adjourned to avoid the passage of legislation which he opposed, such actions were clear evidence that the President claimed unilateral authority to assume or to countermand the legislative power of Congress. Moreover, the selective enforcement of laws was a direct negation of his constitutional responsibility to "take care that the laws be faithfully executed."

These actions led to a large number of cases in the federal courts, almost all of which went against the executive,[50] though few were decided by the Supreme Court. The steel-seizure case proved to be a useful precedent for the courts at all levels, both with respect to questions of inherent executive authority and over the division of power between the President and Congress. The Supreme Court slowly but surely was drawn into the political conflict because increasingly its constitutional authority, and that of the judicial process, was challenged by the Nixon administration. This was reflected in the decision in *United States v. U.S. District Court* (1972)[51] where Justice Powell, the new Nixon appointee from the South, rejected administration claims, based on legislation in 1968, that the President had the inherent power to order wiretaps in domestic security matters without judicial authorization.

It is ironic that defenders of a "strict construction" of the Constitution, and the strongest critics of the Warren Court in Congress such as Senator Sam Ervin of North Carolina, now found it necessary to seek judicial support in defending congressional authority in domestic affairs from executive actions. A Supreme Court which Nixon had tried to influence to assume a new role was obliged to delineate the limits of inherent executive authority and privilege in order to protect judicial procedures and the Constitution. It was over the Nixon interpretation of "executive privilege" as it related to the investigations that followed the Watergate break-in of July 1972 that the Supreme Court had a decisive impact on political events.

Executive privilege was not a new doctrine, but its constitutional basis was shaky.[52] In his first term Nixon personally invoked executive privilege on four occasions, resurrecting arguments made (but not accepted) during the Eisenhower administration that the President had "uncontrolled discretion" to keep executive information from Congress. Moreover, Nixon sought to extend this privilege to White House staff and to documentary information. When the committee headed by Senator Ervin investigating the Watergate break-in and other presidential campaign activities were told in June 1973 of the existence of taped conversations between President Nixon and his staff, they requested access to potentially relevant tapes. The President rejected the request, citing the need for confidentiality of presidential communications and papers, and the committee served two subpoenas on the President, calling for tape recordings of specific conversations. More significantly, the grand jury considering allegations made by one of the men convicted of the Watergate break-in requested the White House to produce specific tapes to help them with their investigations. When the White House refused to produce the tapes, the grand jury directed the Watergate Special Prosecutor Archibald Cox to subpoena the materials. The White House refused to comply with either subpoena, claiming with respect to the latter that the President was not subject "to compulsory process from the courts."

The Ervin Committee brought suit against the President, but Judge Sirica of the U.S. District Court in Washington, D.C., ruled that Congress had provided no statutory basis for the suit, and the court had no jurisdiction to hear it.[53] The Court of Appeals later ruled that the Ervin Committee did not need the tapes to perform its duties. The subpoena on behalf of the grand jury, however, was considered favourably by Sirica, who directed the President to turn over the tapes to him for private inspection so that he could decide whether their contents were protected by executive privilege. Both sides appealed against the Sirica opinion, and in *Nixon v. Sirica*[54] the U.S. Court of Appeals for the District of Columbia Circuit upheld Sirica's directive, making it clear that the President must obey a court order. This case was never appealed to the Supreme Court. In an attempt to escape compliance with the district court's order President Nixon fired Watergate Special Prosecutor Cox, who had refused to accept a compromise whereby Nixon would prepare a statement based on the subpoenaed tapes which would be verified by a Senator and then submitted to Judge Sirica. The "firestorm" which followed Nixon's action and the resignations of the Attorney General and his Deputy in protest, forced Nixon to announce that he would comply with the subpoena. Later it was disclosed that two of the subpoenaed tapes did not exist, and that there were gaps in other tapes.

In November 1973 the President appointed a new Special Prosecutor, Leon Jaworski, and in January 1974 announced that he had voluntarily provided him with all the material necessary to conclude investigations. In February the House of Representatives initiated possible impeachment proceedings against the President. In March the Watergate grand jury indicted several former members of the Nixon administration for conspiracy and obstruction of justice in the Watergate cover-up, and named Nixon as an unindicted co-conspirator. In April, Jaworski asked Sirica to issue a subpoena for sixty-four tapes of White House conversations and other papers which he believed were necessary to produce a case against the Watergate cover-up defendants. Sirica issued a subpoena, ordering the President to produce these materials for judicial inspection to determine their relevance. White House attorneys asked that the subpoena be withdrawn, arguing that the President was immune from such orders. Nixon personally invoked executive privilege as protection against the subpoena, claiming that further disclosures "would be contrary to the public interest." Sirica denied the request, rejecting both the argument that the courts could not resolve such an issue and the claim for an absolute executive privilege. The President sought review in the court of appeals, but Jaworski filed a petition directly to the Supreme Court. The Court accepted it, citing the steel-seizure case as a precedent for resolving the question promptly, and agreed to hear the case of *United States v. Richard M. Nixon*.[55]

Quite apart from the remarkable situation at the time, with the

President under threat of impeachment, the Court's decision was unavoidable but risky. Both before and after oral argument before the Court, the spokesmen for the President refused to affirm that he would obey an order to turn over the tapes. The implication remained that if the President did not agree with the "guidance" given by the Court, he might not feel obliged to obey its ruling. This may account for the fact that the Court came to a unanimous opinion, and gave special emphasis to the obligations of public officials to preserve the integrity of the criminal-justice system.

Hence a Court containing four Nixon appointees had little hesitation in re-affirming that it was the duty of the courts to state what the law is. The Court opinion delivered by Chief Justice Burger rejected the President's contention that the issue was an intra-branch dispute, and asserted that the Special Prosecutor had standing to bring the case, that a justiciable controversy existed, and that the Special Prosecutor had made a strong enough case to justify a subpoena before the actual trial. The Court considered the claim that the separation-of-powers doctrine precluded judicial review of the President's claim of privilege, and affirmed that such a claim of absolute privilege, if invoked regarding a criminal prosecution, would itself violate the separation of powers by preventing the judiciary from performing its duties. Citing the steel-seizure precedent, the Court claimed that it had held other exercises of executive authority unconstitutional and it could not permit the President to be his own judge of executive privilege. The Court emphasized the interdependence as well as the separateness of the branches of government. Neither separation of powers nor confidentiality could sustain an absolute presidential privilege of immunity from the judicial process in all circumstances. "Absent a claim of need to protect military, diplomatic or sensitive national security secrets", the Court could not accept that the production of presidential communications for *in camera* inspection by the district court would significantly diminish confidentiality. The Court asserted that in this situation, relating to a possible criminal case involving executive officials, their judgement of the public interest should prevail over that of the President: "The generalized assertion of privilege must yield to the demonstrated, specific need for evidence in a pending criminal trial." Referring to Chief Justice Marshall's views in the *Burr* case, the Court went on to reaffirm the need for the district court to give presidential communications special protection and confidentiality, but they were in no doubt that the President should provide the material requested.

Hence the Supreme Court established that presidential com-

munications in certain specific situations did not enjoy absolute
privilege, while conceding that in certain other circumstances such
a privilege might exist. In this sense it was a major defeat for
President Nixon, but not necessarily for the Presidency, especially
with respect to dealings with Congress. Its immediate effect was
to force the President to give up certain tapes, which in turn
prompted the House of Representatives to draw up articles of
impeachment. The public release of three tapes that Nixon was
now compelled to turn over to Sirica clearly revealed his participa-
tion in the cover-up. Faced with certain impeachment, and
probable conviction and removal from office, Nixon resigned on
August 8th, 1974. Any doubts as to the authority of Court
decisions were consigned by Watergate to the same fate as befell
President Nixon.

6: Epilogue

The Nixon Presidency revealed that the Court remains an important check on 'revolutionary' executive initiatives in the area
of domestic affairs. It also suggests that the Court is singularly
difficult to control through the appointment process. The Court
has had little opportunity but also little apparent incentive to re-
strain the Presidency with respect to foreign affairs and national
security, and may even have delineated an area where executive
privilege might be legitimate. Hence, while the Court may have
helped to create the modern Presidency, it still exerts a potent if
erratic influence on the parameters of presidential authority.
Moreover, one of the significant factors in *United States v. Nixon*
was Nixon's challenge to judicial review, and with specific reference to *Marbury v. Madison* the Court re-emphasized its duty to
uphold the law and the Constitution. The Court can also take
political initiatives in furtherance of its perceived responsibilities,
but such action is likely to be controversial and also inconsistent
with the canons of practice it has required of Congress and the
President.

The main areas of interaction between the President and the
Court include judicial appointments and the delicate issue of
court-packing, acceptance of the Court's interpretation of the
Constitution as expressed in judicial review, and executive compliance with, and enforcement or non-enforcement of, judicial

decisions. In consequence the Court, like Congress or the President, can at times be portrayed as the saviour of the Republic, or the usurper of authority vested elsewhere. An important difference, however, is that the Court is a non-elected body. This may be desirable for a supreme judicial body, but if the Court can legitimately claim to be the "ultimate interpreter" of the Constitution as it relates to the authority conferred on the elected branches of government, it behoves the Court to resist the temptation to make policies.

The evidence suggests that, after the confrontation with Franklin Roosevelt and up to 1968, the Court was in tune with public opinion in giving limited support to the executive. It combined a sensitivity to the burdens of responsibility for foreign policy and national security with the courage to set limits on executive authority at home if it infringed or usurped legislative or judicial powers. Executive abuses of authority in foreign affairs may be as much the result of congressional cowardice as of benign judicial neglect.

Two persistent trends stand out. The first is the extent to which the Court, sometimes against its best judicial instincts, has legitimized expansions of national governmental and executive authority deemed to be necessary political responses to particular situations; in effect, it has tried to balance constitutional stability and the constitutional change consistent with shifts in public attitudes and political demands. The second trend is the will to limit or refine the scope of such expansion if it is challenged as conflicting with basic constitutional principles or might interfere with the judicial process itself. Both of these trends were evident in the example set by Chief Justice Marshall. If there has been any consistency of approach, it has been in the interpretation of the separation of powers as a formal separation requiring comity and co-operation between institutions if it is to work, but on occasions leading to political conflicts which must be decided ultimately by judicial decisions. Such decisions will include judgements about the legitimate scope of national governmental authority as well as the authority of particular institutions.

The behaviour of the Court towards the Presidency since 1933 has been in accord with the 'creative tension' built into the Constitution by the combination of the separation of institutions and a system of checks and balances. The President may act, but the Court provides an opportunity to check such action — and who prevails may depend in the end on public opinion. On most occasions major issues are resolved by the President and Congress, but the former depends more than the latter on the Court to legitimize any extensions of authority. In foreign affairs and times of 'war' the Court, for good or ill, has rarely embarrassed Presidents. Where particular Presidents have claimed authority or privileges at home which have been challenged as infringements on or a negation of the constitutional obligations of other branches of government, the Court has been less charitably disposed. Hence the state of the Presidency in the future, as in the past, will be conditioned by the potential impact of Supreme Court decisions.

Guide to Further Reading

There are many general and specific books on the Supreme Court and on the Presidency. This guide is intended to suggest material which will amplify the particular relationships discussed in the text. In order to understand the Court, there is no substitute for reading the Court's own opinions; hence specific citations have been given, in the Notes, to the *United States Reports* (U.S.), the *Federal Reporter, Second Series* (F.2d), and *Federal Supplement* (F.Supp.). The classic study of the Court up to 1918 is Charles Warren, *The Supreme Court in United States History,* 2 vols. (1922; rev. ed., Boston: Little, Brown, 1926). A detailed historical analysis is provided by Alfred H. Kelly and Winfred A. Harbison, *The American Constitution: Its Origins and Development* (New York: W. W. Norton, 1948; rev. eds., 1955, 1970). Perhaps the most valuable historical summary is Robert G. McCloskey, *The American Supreme Court* (Chicago: Chicago UP, 1960). A short but succinct introduction to the contemporary Court is Archibald Cox, *The Role of the Supreme Court in American Government* (New York: Oxford UP, 1976), while Robert H. Jackson, *The Supreme Court in the American System of Government* (New York: Harper & Row, 1963), is a cogent statement by a respected member of the Court. A most useful general study of the Court is Richard Funston's *A Vital National Seminar* (1978).[6]*

The classic constitutional work on the Presidency remains Edward Corwin's *The President: Office and Powers* (1940; 4th ed., 1958).[29] Among the many studies of the contemporary Presidency, the following are probably the most useful in helping to understand its various facets: Louis Koenig, *The Chief Executive* (New York: Harcourt, Brace, Jovanovich, 3rd ed., 1975), Thomas E. Cronin, *The State of the Presidency* (Boston: Little, Brown, 1974), and Arthur Schlesinger, Jr., *The Imperial Presidency* (1974).[2]

Two books deal directly with relations between the Supreme Court and the Presidency: Glendon A. Schubert, Jr., *The Presidency in the Courts* (Minneapolis: Minnesota UP, 1957), and Robert Scigliano, *The Supreme Court and the Presidency* (1971);[4] the latter is more historically based and includes a perceptive dis-

---

* *For full bibliographical details, see the appropriate reference in the Notes as indicated.*

cussion of appointments and performances in the light of presidential expectations. On judicial appointments, the major general
work is Henry J. Abraham, *Justice and Presidents: A Political
History of Appointments to the Supreme Court* (New York:
Oxford UP, 1974). Studies of specific aspects of the selection process include Joseph P. Harris, *The Advice and Consent of the
Senate* (Berkeley: California UP, 1953), and Joel B. Grossman,
*Lawyers and Judges: The ABA and the Politics of Judicial Selec-
tion* (New York: Wiley, 1965), while David J. Danelski, *A
Supreme Court Justice is Appointed* (New York: Random House,
1964), is an excellent case-study of the appointment of Butler
in 1922 — and provides an interesting comparison to the discussion of the Carswell nomination in Richard Harris, *Decision* (New
York: E.P. Dutton, 1971). The Fortas affair is assessed in Robert
Shogan, *A Question of Judgment* (Indianapolis: Bobbs-Merrill,
1972).

Most text books on the Supreme Court discuss judicial review
and the concept of "political questions", but detailed analysis
can be obtained from Alexander M. Bickel, *The Least Dangerous
Branch: The Supreme Court at the Bar of Politics* (Indianapolis:
Bobbs-Merrill, 1962), and Phillipa Strum, *The Supreme Court
and "Political Questions": A Study in Judicial Evasion* (University,
Ala.: Alabama UP, 1974). A good summary case against judicial
review is made in Charles S. Hyneman, *The Supreme Court on
Trial* (New York: Atherton Press, 1963), Pt. 2, and a trenchant
attack in Louis B. Boudin, *Government by Judiciary*, 2 vols.
(New York: William Goodwin, 1932).

The conflict between Franklin Roosevelt and the Court has
been assessed from a number of perspectives. Edward S. Corwin,
Constitutional Revolution, Ltd. (Pomona, Cal.: Claremont
Colleges, 1941), discusses the changing constitutional doctrines
and their acceptance by the Court after 1937. Stimulating analysis
of the Court in the 1930s and 1940s is contained in C. Herman
Pritchett's *The Roosevelt Court* (1948)[20] and Alpheus T. Mason's
The Supreme Court from Taft to Burger (1979).[18] Joseph Alsop
and Turner Catledge, *The 168 Days* (Garden City, N.Y.: Doubleday
Doran, 1938), is a contemporary account of the Court-packing
struggle, while Robert H. Jackson's *The Struggle for Judicial
Supremacy* (New York: Knopf, 1941) assesses the crisis from the
viewpoint of a protagonist of the President. The drama of the
event is well portrayed in James M. Burns, *Roosevelt: The Lion
and the Fox* (New York: Harcourt, Brace, 1956), while William
Leuchtenburg's essays (1966, 1969)[19] provide new insights into
the Court-packing plan. The Roosevelt-Hughes clash and the later

influence of Stone is put into a historical context in Alpheus T. Mason, *The Supreme Court: Palladium of Freedom* (Ann Arbor: Michigan UP, 1962).

Maeva Marcus, *Truman and the Steel Seizure Case* (1977),[30] is an exhaustive study which also assesses the implications of the case for the Presidency today, and has an extensive bibliography, while Alan F. Westin, *The Anatomy of a Constitutional Law Case* (New York: Macmillan, 1958), is another valuable study of the case. Clinton Rossiter, *The Supreme Court and the Commander in Chief* (1951),[29] provides important information on the Court's handling of 'war' problems, and is also available with additional text on the more recent period by Richard P. Longaker (Ithaca, N.Y.: Cornell UP, 1976).

The Warren Court has been the subject of a range of studies, some supportive, others critical. Among the best of the former is Archibald Cox, *The Warren Court: Constitutional Decision as an Instrument of Reform* (Cambridge, Mass.: Harvard UP, 1968). Mildly critical and eminently readable is Philip Kurland, *Politics, the Constitution and the Warren Court* (1970).[42] Alexander M. Bickel, *The Supreme Court and the Idea of Progress* (New York: Harper & Row, 1970), is a thoughtful critique, while Richard Funston's *Constitutional Counterrevolution?* (1977)[43] is a detailed and controversial commentary on the Court under Warren and Burger.

The *Brown* case is analysed in great detail and with much literary panache in Richard Kluger's *Simple Justice* (1976),[36] which also has extensive bibliographical information. The consequences of this decision are analysed in detail in J. Harvie Wilkinson III, *From Brown to Bakke. The Supreme Court and School Integration: 1954-1978* (New York: Oxford UP, 1979), while the style and attitudes of the Warren Court are criticized in Richard Maidment's articles (1975, 1977)[35] and in Raoul Berger, *Government by Judiciary: The Transformation of the Fourteenth Amendment* (Cambridge, Mass.: Harvard UP, 1977). The difficulties of implementing the decision are discussed in Jack Peltason's *Fifty-Eight Lonely Men* (1961).[37] For executive reactions to civil rights issues, Ruth P. Morgan, *The President and Civil Rights* (New York: St. Martin's Press, 1970), is brief but useful.

The Court's reticence regarding the war in Vietnam is analysed critically in Anthony D'Amato and Robert O'Neil, *The Judiciary and Vietnam* (1972),[48] and the President's claims to war-making authority challenged in Jacob Javits, *Who Makes War* (New York: Morrow, 1973). The attempt by Nixon to 'pack' the judiciary is discussed in detail in James Simon's *In His Own Image* (1973),[44] though the analysis is rather shaky. Raoul Berger's *Executive Privilege* (1974)[52] is a devastating and scrupulously documented attack on the myth of executive privilege.

Several sources provide detailed discussion of the legal consequences of Watergate. The five-volume collection edited by A. Stephen Boyan, Jr., *Constitutional Aspects of Watergate: Documents and Materials* (Dobbs Ferry, N.Y.: Oceana Publications, 1976-79), contains extensive information on executive privilege and other legal issues. The crucial role of the federal courts in the Watergate affair is examined in Howard Ball, *No Pledge of Privacy: The Watergate Tapes Litigation* (Port Washington, N.Y.: Kennikat Press, 1977), while the documentary material on *United States v. Nixon,* including the oral argument before the Supreme Court, is available in Leon Friedman, ed., *United States v. Nixon: The President Before the Supreme Court* (New York: Chelsea House, 1974). The related congressional investigations are examined in James Hamilton, *The Power to Probe: A Study of Congressional Investigations* (New York: Random House, 1976), and a stimulating assessment of the constitutional crisis is contained in Philip Kurland, *Watergate and the Constitution* (1978).[3]

Notes

1. See Ira H. Carmen, *Power and Balance: An Introduction to American Constitutional Government* (New York: Harcourt Brace Jovanovich, 1978), pp. 170-224.

2. Arthur M. Schlesinger Jr., *The Imperial Presidency* (Boston: Houghton Mifflin, 1973, and London: Andre Deutsch, 1974).

3. See Philip B. Kurland, *Watergate and the Constitution* (Chicago: Chicago UP, 1978).

4. Robert Scigliano, *The Supreme Court and the Presidency* (New York: Free Press, 1971).

5. *Marbury v. Madison,* 5 U.S. (1 Cranch) 137. This standard form of notation refers to the *United States Reports,* vol. 5, p. 137, though for the early years of the Court the volumes are often referred to by the name of the current official Reporter, in this case William Cranch's first volume.

6. On the significance of judicial review, see Richard Y. Funston, *A Vital National Seminar: The Supreme Court in American National Life* (Palo Alto, Cal.: Mayfield Publishing Co., 1978), pp. 1-32.

7. Scigliano, p. 35.

8. Arguably, this was true even in the so-called "Progressive era": see J.A. Thompson, *Progressivism*, the second pamphlet in this series, esp. pp. 39-40.

9. *In re Neagle*, 135 U.S. 1.

10. *In re Debs*, 158 U.S. 564.

11. *Myers v. United States*, 272 U.S. 52.

12. See Harris Warren, *Herbert Hoover and the Great Depression* (New York: Oxford UP, 1959). For the New Deal period, see William E. Leuchtenburg, *Franklin D. Roosevelt and the New Deal, 1932-1940* (New York: Harper & Row, 1963).

13. 293 U.S. 388.

14. *Schechter v. United States*, 295 U.S. 495.

15. 295 U.S. 602. The decision was qualified later in *Morgan v. Tennessee Valley Authority*, 312 U.S. 701 (1941).

16. 297 U.S. 1.

17. *Carter v. Carter Coal Co.*, 298 U.S. 238.

18. Alpheus T. Mason, *The Supreme Court from Taft to Burger* (Baton Rouge: Louisiana State UP, 1979), p. 97. This is a revised and enlarged edition of id., *The Supreme Court from Taft to Warren* (ibid., 1958).

19. W.E. Leuchtenburg, "The Origins of Franklin D. Roosevelt's 'Court-Packing' Plan," in Philip B. Kurland, ed., *The Supreme Court Review, 1966* (Chicago: Chicago UP, 1966), pp. 347-400. See also id., "Franklin D. Roosevelt's Supreme Court 'Packing' Plan," in Harold M. Hollingsworth and William F. Holmes, eds., *Essays on the New Deal* (Austin: Texas UP, 1969).

20. C. Herman Pritchett, *The Roosevelt Court. A Study in Judicial Politics and Values, 1937-1947* (Chicago: Quadrangle, 1948).

21. 304 U.S. 104.

22. 67 U.S. (2 Black) 635.

23. *United States v. Curtiss-Wright Export Corporation*, 299 U.S. 304.

24. In *United States v. Belmont*, 301 U.S. 304 (1937), and *United States v. Pink*, 315 U.S. 203 (1942), the Court tacitly accepted that executive agreements with foreign governments, entered into by the President alone, could be enforced in the courts as internal law, and hence be legally analogous to treaties.

25. 17 Fed. Cases 144 (No. 9487).

26. *Hirabayashi v. United States*, 320 U.S. 81 (1943); *Korematsu v. United States*, 323 U.S. 214 (1944); *Ex parte Endo*, 323 U.S. 283 (1944). Also in 1944 the Court by a narrow majority reversed a conviction under the Espionage Act of 1917 *(Hartzel v. United States*, 322 U.S. 680).

27. 341 U.S. 494.

28. 343 U.S. 579 (1952).

29. See Edward S. Corwin, *The President: Office and Powers, 1787-1948* (1940; 3rd ed. rev., New York: New York UP, 1948); C.H. Pritchett, "The President and the Supreme Court," *Journal of Politics*, 11 (1949), 80-92; and Clinton Rossiter, *The Supreme Court and the Commander in Chief* (1951; rept., New York: Da Capo Press, 1970).

30. For the background to the case and analysis of the written opinions, see Maeva Marcus, *Truman and the Steel Seizure Case: The Limits of Presidential Power* (New York: Columbia UP, 1977), pp. 102-227.

31. Schlesinger, *Imperial Presidency*, p. 143.

32. For the outcome of the steel dispute, see Marcus, pp. 249-56.

33. 347 U.S. 483.

34. *Plessy v. Ferguson*, 163 U.S. 537.

35. See R.A. Maidment, "Changing Styles in Constitutional Adjudication: The United States Supreme Court and Racial Segregation," *Public Law* (1977), 168-86, and id., "Policy in Search of Law: the Warren Court from *Brown* to *Miranda*," *Journal of American Studies*, 9 (1975), 301-20.

36. See Richard Kluger, *Simple Justice* (New York: Knopf, 1976, and London: Andre Deutsch, 1977).

37. See Robbins L. Gates, *The Making of Massive Resistance* (Chapel Hill: North Carolina UP, 1964), and Jack W. Peltason, *Fifty-Eight Lonely Men* (New York: Harcourt, Brace, 1961).

38. *Cooper v. Aaron*, 358 U.S. 1, and *Griffin v. County School Board of Prince Edward County*, 377 U.S. 218.

39. See *Baker v. Carr*, 369 U.S. 186 (1962).

40. See in particular *Yates v. United States*, 345 U.S. 298 (1957). In the 1960s the emphasis shifted to the defence of the rights of criminal defendants and religious minorities.

41. M. Shapiro, "The Supreme Court: From Warren to Burger," in Anthony King, ed., *The New American Political System* (Washington D.C.: American Enterprise Institute, 1978), p. 193.

42. For development of these arguments, see Philip B. Kurland, *Politics, the Constitution and the Warren Court* (Chicago and London: Chicago UP, 1970), pp. 21-50 and 98-169.

43. Richard Y. Funston, *Constitutional Counterrevolution? The Warren Court and the Burger Court: Judicial Policy Making in Modern America* (Cambridge, Mass.: Schenkman, 1977), pp. 297-325.

44. For a different interpretation, see James F. Simon, *In His Own Image: The Supreme Court in Richard Nixon's America* (New York: McKay, 1973).

45. *Alexander v. Holmes County Board of Education*, 396 U.S. 19, and *Swann v. Charlotte-Mecklenburg Board of Education*, 402 U.S. 1.

46. Schlesinger, *Imperial Presidency*, Ch. 8.

47. Ibid., p. 252.

48. See Anthony A. D'Amato and Robert M. O'Neil, *The Judiciary and Vietnam* (New York: St. Martin's Press, 1972).

49. *New York Times v. United States,* 403 U.S. 713 (1971).

50. On impoundment, see *Train v. City of New York,* 420 U.S. 35 (1975), and *City of New York v. Ruckelshaus,* 385 F. Supp. 669 (D.D.C. 1973); on the pocket-veto power, see *Kennedy v. Sampson,* 511 F.2d 430 (D.C. Circ. 1974); on the dismantling of the Office of Economic Opportunity, see *Williams v. Phillips,* 360 F. Supp. 1363 (D.D.C. 1973).

51. 407 U.S. 297. This decision was reinforced in *United States v. Giordano,* 416 U.S. 505 (1974).

52. See Raoul Berger, *Executive Privilege: A Constitutional Myth* (Cambridge, Mass.: Harvard UP, 1974).

53. *Senate Select Committee on Presidential Campaign Activities v. Nixon,* 366 F. Supp. 51 (D.D.C. 1973).

54. 487 F.2d 700 (D.C. Cir. 1973).

55. 418 U.S. 683 (1974).